# Hands Are Not
# for Hitting

# Hands come in all shapes, colours, and sizes.

# Hands can do lots of things.
## Can you wave yours?

Hands are not for hitting.
What are hands for?

Saying hello

# Drawing

Playing

the incy-wincy spider...

Building

Hands are not for hitting.
What are hands for?

Eating and drinking

Dressing

# Keeping safe

Taking care

Hands are not for hitting.
What are hands for?

Helping

Hugging

# Waving

# Tips for Parents and Caregivers

Toddlers want to touch and pick up just about anything they can reach (and most things they can't!). Toddlers start to gain a sense of self as they discover many of the powerful things their hands can do – throw balls, pour juice, open containers, play with new toys, "read" books, and more. Learning new things is exciting, but it can also be frustrating when their little hands can't do everything they want. When toddlers get angry and frustrated, they're quick to learn another powerful thing their hands can do: hit.

The majority of toddlers will go through a phase where they hit. We can teach them that feeling angry is okay, but hitting is not. Most often, toddlers hit when they feel strong emotions that they have trouble expressing through words. Watch for signs that a child may be angry, frustrated, tired, grumpy, or distressed and encourage using words to express emotions as a step to avoid hitting. You can help toddlers learn to name their feelings. Try, "I can see that you're angry. Your friend tore your book and that makes you mad." Or, "Uh-oh! Your book is torn. Are you angry about that?" Help the toddler resolve the situation that caused the anger or frustration. Remind him or her, "No matter how mad we get, it's never okay to hit. Hitting hurts." Then help the child to redirect the anger in a safe way.

## Suggestions for redirecting frustrated energy

Breathe! Together, close your eyes and take deep breaths, telling the child to suck in as much air as possible and then blow it out, as if blowing out the candles on a birthday cake.

Play "Superhands." Talk about the good, helpful things that Superhands can do. Superhands can fly to the rescue and save the day by putting away toys, feeding a pet, or giving a high five or a hug to someone who needs a smile.

Clap. A popular tool in preschools and childcare settings to get children's attention is to clap the chant "1-2-3, eyes on me." Children stop what they're doing and join in the chant.

## Intervening when a toddler hits

In most cases, focus first on the child who has been hit. If necessary, gently but firmly separate the children so the child who hit will not do it again, saying, "Hands are not for hitting. Hitting hurts." Ask the child who hit to apologise to the other child. Help both children resolve the situation that led to the hitting. It's not appropriate to slap or spank a child as a consequence of hitting – doing this will hurt and confuse the child.

Keep in mind that toddlers are just beginning to learn socially acceptable behavior. Teaching and redirecting is a process you may need to repeat over and over. Reinforcing the ideas in *Hands Are Not for Hitting* can help children begin to safely handle anger and frustration and to discover the many fun and useful things they can do with their hands.

First published in the UK in 2008 by Bloomsbury Publishing Plc
50 Bedford Square, London, WC1B 3DP

www.bloomsbury.com

Bloomsbury is a registered trademark of Bloomsbury Publishing Plc

ISBN 978-1-4081-1071-3

A CIP catalogue record for this book is available at the British Library.

Original edition © 2006 by Free Spirit Publishing Inc., Minneapolis, Minnesota, U.S.A., http://www.freespirit.com under the title: Best Behavior: Hands are not for Hitting.
All rights reserved under International and Pan-American Copyright Conventions.

Printed in China by Leo Paper Products

This book is produced using paper that is made from wood grown in well-managed forests. It is natural, renewable and recyclable. The logging and manufacturing processes conform to the environmental regulations of the country of origin.